T0413528

Fall, Learn, Rise

Aryo Hadi

AuthorHouse™ UK Ltd.
500 Avebury Boulevard
Central Milton Keynes, MK9 2BE
www.authorhouse.co.uk
Phone: 08001974150

First published by AuthorHouse   02/26/2011

ISBN: 978-1-4567-7511-7 (sc)
ISBN; 978-1-4567-7512-4 (hc)
ISBN: 978-1-4567-7513-1 (e)

Preface

The author wishes to express gratitude to the reader for choosing this book. Whether it was chosen for the interest in the issue of adolescents' true to life experiences in Japan, or because of the desire to lend a helping hand to his charity project, it is his greatest wish to make this reading experience fulfilling.

In life, we all experience hard times that bring us down or make us feel as if we want to give up. Now and then, we do give up. However, the greatest chance to find another approach is after making sure that one has given it his all and that the moment has come to lay down his sword. On the other hand, there are those occasions when one conquers his enemies to claim the crown of victory. How great that feels! That is why the author is sharing this book of real kids who tackle troubles facing them with all their might. Even when they fall, they manage to arise time and again with the resolve that today is the day to win.

The book is like a car, and words like a window looking into someone's life. It is the author's hope that the drive through different stories provides insight into how to solve the reader's own problems. Knowing that one is not alone and those others before him have emerged triumphant against their obstacles can be inspirational.

The young contributors of these stories are all adolescents of different nationalities and backgrounds living in Japan. They prevailed over their challenges and found their own special solutions.

So no matter how daunting the prospect is for someone to get up and face another day, if one does his best he will have no regrets. Never back down.

Acknowledgements

I could not have made this book without the help of a number of people who all contributed in their own ways. First and foremost, I would like to express gratitude to my parents for believing in me; to my mother, who made the arrangements with the publisher and the charity organizations. I am very thankful for her assistance for without which I could not have made this book. I want to thank my father, who always gives me love and support, and inspired me to make this book.

I am grateful to my homeroom teacher, Noel Southall, who guided me in this project and gave me great ideas. His support and opinions helped in different parts of the book writing process. Special thanks to Mr. Schneider, the Secondary School Principal, who gave me permission to do this project and send out information to the school community. I'd like to thank Miss Cussen, my English teacher, who encouraged students in her class to share their true story for this book.

I wish to thank all my friends who contributed their stories to the book. It is extremely difficult to open up about one's weaknesses in front of the whole world. They decided to lend a hand to my project for a greater cause. I commend them for their bravery and desire to help others.

I would like to give a heartfelt thanks to Mrs. Hiromi Okouchi, who translated the whole book into Japanese. I sincerely appreciate your patience and hard work. I would not have been able to do this project without you.

Finally, I cannot emphasize enough how grateful I am to everyone who bought this book; it means a lot to me, and the proceeds will go to helping other people have better lives.

Fall, Learn, Rise

If you think that this book could help someone you know with their problems, please tell them about it.

Table of Contents

Preface.. i

Acknowledgements.. iv

1. Allergy Attack.. 1

2. All Because of My Culture.. 10

3. Broken Heart.. 18

4. My US Experience... 22

5. Where Do I Belong?.. 28

6. Living as a Minority in Japan 34

7. Together Forever... 40

8. Teacher Trouble... 46

9. My Fear of Public Speaking 50

About the Charity Organization Gawad Kalinga 54

転んで、学んで、立ち上がる―日本語版....................... 57

はじめに.. 58

謝辞.. 61

1. アレルギー発作.. 64

2. すべては文化のせいで.. 74

3. 心の中にある傷.. 82

4. 僕のアメリカ体験.. 87

5. 私は何者？ **94**

6. マイノリティとして生きる **101**

7. ずっと一緒に **107**

8. 先生こわい **113**

9. 人前で話すこと恐怖症 **117**

慈善団体ガワド・カリンガについて...............................**122**

'It is hard to fail, but it is worse never to have tried to succeed.'

Theodore Roosevelt

1

Allergy Attack
(By Aryo, 15 years old)

It all began when I was four months old when I started showing serious symptoms of asthma. It got worse, and I stayed in the hospital most of the time until I reached the age of three. I was on heavy medication constantly. I attended nursery school, but was absent almost every day. On top of that, as I entered primary school, I started to have severe allergic reactions to many kinds of food.

I couldn't eat most sweets because they contained white sugar. I couldn't have junk food because it had oil, fat, and additives that I could not consume. I couldn't have most kinds of bread because they had yeast and wheat, and I couldn't eat cold food because it made me feel sick. I couldn't have milk, rice, and other foods either. My biggest enemy was eggs, the one ingredient prominent in a wide range of foods.

In addition, there was a long list of things I was not able to eat. The list of things I could eat was much shorter than the list of what I could not!

I felt that it wasn't fair that I was the only person in my class who couldn't eat normal food like everyone else. During excursions and birthday parties, my mom always packed me a special allergen free lunch box, and I had to eat that while staring at regular kids eating tasty looking food.

In grade five, I became so weak from my allergies that I couldn't even come to school for long periods of time. I spent most days just lying on the sofa in the living room of my home while my mom made me "allergy food" that tasted plain, as always. Still, I couldn't complain because when I ate or drank something I wasn't supposed to, I had very bad allergic reactions, causing my whole body to have an unrelenting, horrible itch and high fever. I also couldn't play under the sun because it made me break out in rashes. My whole body became inflamed and it hurt when my skin came in contact with my clothes. My face and body had layers of different shades of pink and red because my skin was trying to heal but couldn't because I kept scratching it even in my sleep. I always felt pity in people's eyes when they looked at me. I was sad every day because I thought I would never be a normal kid, never get cured.

My parents had me regularly checked by doctors to find out what was wrong but the results never showed anything clear. I just kept on getting more medicine.

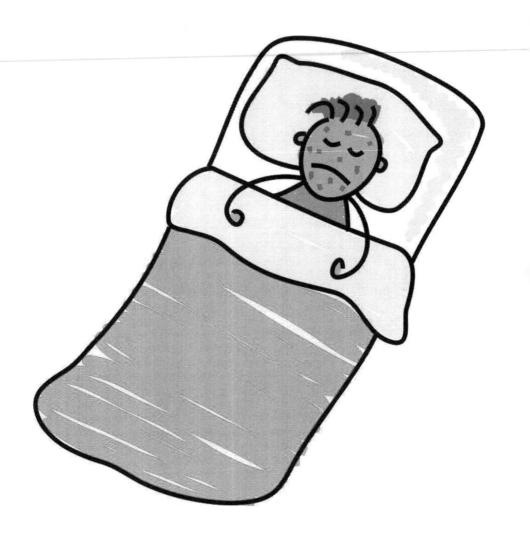

I felt tired every day, physically and mentally. My parents could tell that my treatments were not working, so the first big step that changed everything was resetting my whole lifestyle including food, sleep habits, and exercise.

I only ate the food I knew was safe while completely avoiding other food. Also, I stopped using steroids and other medicines for my allergies because their habitual use had only worsened my health. I had been using an ointment on my skin that hid the angry rashes and red wounds from my fingernails, which searched constantly for places to scratch. However, this ointment only concealed the wounds, so it did nothing to cure me.

After I stopped using it, my skin initially got very red and itchy again, but I eventually started getting better. A macrobiotic dietician, a chiropractor, and my mom, who learned naturopathy along the way, helped me increase the food I could eat gradually, rebalance my body, and advised me on how to reboot my whole system and start anew. It was a long process, and there were many ups and downs along the way.

I still remember very clearly the first morning that I woke up and realized that I had slept soundly through the night. I jumped out of bed without any help, and ran downstairs to greet my family a "Good Morning!" I think this moment was when I first realized that I was going to get better. It was as if a smile was creeping into my face everyday, and that smile kept getting bigger and bigger until I felt like nothing could stop me.

I could attend school more frequently, play outside in the sunny weather, sleep well at night, and eat food that had been forbidden for a long time. Finally, after three years, I was completely better and looking at a bright future where anything could happen, where I could do anything I wanted. I went through a lot of hard times when I just wanted to crawl into a ball and give up, but my family and friends supported me all the way. It is they who made me the way I am now. I will never forget the hard days I had, but all my loved ones showed me the way, the bright side of my life.

I am forever indebted to my parents, who always believed in me no matter what. My mom, especially took care of me every single day without fail. My dad, worked hard for the family in spite of the list of things he had to do when he got home from work to help take care of me. They took turns watching over me at night, and my mom searched high and low to find ways to help me get better. My dad carried me around the house, mostly to the toilet because I was too weak to walk by myself. They both comforted me when I was feeling worse than usual. My little sister tried to hide in the kitchen when eating her food, so I wouldn't feel bad seeing her enjoy things I couldn't.

After my ordeal, I realized that I couldn't remember the worst part of my allergy days. It's like there is a blank spot in my memory during the months in grade five when I looked and felt the worst. I think it was a way for my mind to protect its sanity, as I was but a little child back then. I later researched about this condition and came to the conclusion that

I may have a mild case of dissociative amnesia, which causes traumatic or extremely stressful experiences to be buried in the back of the mind. This fact doesn't mean that I don't remember my whole childhood; it just means I don't have memories of most of the period of time when my health was failing. My parents filled me in on what happened after I got better, but I still don't recall some parts of it.

After that experience, I had a clean slate, another chance to turn my life around. I took it, and here I am now, a normal kid with big dreams. Now I can eat anything I want, and physically, it's as if I never had any allergies at all. The trials I faced made me stronger, and I realized how to appreciate life and the importance of believing in your own inner strength. I wish luck to you, whoever you are, in accomplishing your goals and overcoming whatever stands in your way. I hope my story inspired you to do your best no matter what.

Fall, Learn, Rise

'Although the world is full of suffering, it is full also of the over-coming of it.'

Helen Keller

2

All Because of My Culture
(By Qing Tian, 14 years old)

It was English class on another cloudy day, and my classmates and I sat down again to take notes, read books, and discuss topics. However, in today's class, my teacher announced that we would be reading a set of papers entitled "'Third Culture Kids'".

Third Culture Kids, I thought to myself, *isn't this something like myself, something like my past, present, and future?*

As I read the document, it reminded me of a series of events that happened at my previous school. It seemed like just a few days prior, and it all happened because of my culture.

*

First of all, let me give you a bit of detail about myself. I was actually born here in Tokyo, Japan, but my parents are from Shanghai, China. When I was around one, I traveled overseas to China to live with my Chinese grandparents for the next eight years.

In 2005, I flew to Tokyo, Japan once more, although I have no memory of being in such a strange and unfamiliar city. I didn't even know that my nationality was Japanese, and I couldn't even remember what my parents looked like back then. After several months, I managed to learn a bit of Japanese and entered school where everything happened.

It all began when I entered this very first school in Japan when I was in grade five. It was an international school, so I expected that there would be many non-Japanese people there. Indeed, Japanese people were a minority, but what actually stood in majority was just one group of foreigners: South Koreans. I had never met any Koreans in my life until then, and first I was very excited to meet them, study with them, and play around with them. But things eventually changed. A boy called Sun Il appeared in front of me, and the seed of the collision between the South Koreans and I began to sprout.

Sun Il was a short South Korean boy with curly hair, small eyes, and a pointed nose. Somehow, he looked a bit cute. When he was playing with other people, he was very active and playful. One day, I came up to him to greet him as I did other people in the morning. He just peered at me for a second and looked away once more. From that act, I got a small feeling of incongruity, but held it back as I drew a deep breath.

Perhaps he's just too shy, I thought to myself. *After all, he's just a new student like me this year. So, I shall get along with him some day, eventually.* However, that day never arrived.

As the school year moved on, I gradually found Sun Il a bit disturbing. Sometimes he would poke my nose for no reason, and quickly run away. I first thought that he was just pulling a silly prank on me, so I didn't really mind. But then, things got worse. Eventually, Sun Il got brave enough to spit into my ear when I was not looking. He also called some of his South Korean friends over when I was alone to push me down the stairs. One day, I was so concerned about Sun Il that I came up to him during lunch. The homeroom teacher was not there.

"Hey Sun Il," I said, frowning a little. "I want to ask you something,"

He looked up at me slowly and stared for about five seconds. After that, his eyes widened, and the words came out with the force of a typhoon, "Get out of my sight! You Chinese are all pigs!"

I was stunned, and some classmates near us turned around to look. I merely said, "What?" Then, Sun Il and some other South Korean boys started to push me out of the classroom. They were all smaller than me, and I knew that I had more muscles to stand up against all of them combined. Still, I

didn't do anything and allowed the classroom door to slam into my face.

I didn't get it. I couldn't understand why they would do such thing to me for nothing. At least that's what I thought back then. My head was blank as I stared at the door because I knew that such a thing had never happened to me before, and it had happened so suddenly, so quickly. Before I even knew it, I found a tear rolling down my cheek, getting sucked into the carpet beneath my feet.

When I told my mom about what happened that day, she was outraged and irritated. At once, she grabbed a pen and paper and started to write a note that she sent directly to the school office. All that I cared about back then was pretending as though nothing were happening. Little did I know that this incident was just the beginning of a big riot.

When the school office received the note from my mom, they alerted my homeroom teacher to let him sort things out. That day at lunch, my homeroom teacher called all of us over and talked about the event. He mentioned that what Sun Il did was discriminating against Chinese people, which is a terrible thing to do. However, Sun Il opposed the teacher, and gave many reasons why he regarded his actions as right. In addition, every single South Korean, including the ones that were once friendly with me, stood up, pointed, and even shouted at the homeroom teacher, adding to the topic where Sun Il had left off. They enumerated small topics like previous experiences with Chinese people, and moved on to events during WWII, when Chinese people fought against South Koreans during the battle between North and South Korea. The indescribable noise of the arguments even made the school principal rush to our classroom to hear what was going on. He neutralized all the South Koreans by telling them many things about relations between Chinese and Korean people. Some people still protested in front of the principal, but eventually, all went quiet. I didn't speak a word during this big riot, and tears were welling in my eye sockets. The principal talked about the concept of an international school where all children from around the world are welcome. Chinese children are not an exception. He also told all my South Korean classmates that South Korea and China should be friendly, and this type of incident should never happen again. I sighed in relief as the principal left the classroom, and there was a long period of complete silence.

Days later, Sun Il and I, as well as our parents, were all brought to the school office along with the school head office manager, principal, and homeroom teacher, to have a conference about what had happened. During the conference, I finally felt empowered, and explained to everyone how Sun Il had mistreated me before, and how the "riot" had started. Sun Il even protested at that time, pointing at my face. However, he was soon stopped by his mom, and he was silent for the rest of the meeting. All he did was look at me out of the corner of his eye. A week after the meeting, Sun Il was expelled.

The day after Sun Il was expelled, every South Korean in the classroom changed magnificently. They treated me like a normal/good friend, and I was happy for the rest of the school year.

*

I had finished reading the document, and just realized that I was a person like a Third Culture Kid. Even though I was born in Japan and have Japanese citizenship, I presume that most of my ancestors are Chinese. In the school I attend now, I have some South Korean friends, too. Nobody acts like Sun Il anymore. I feel happy about it, and I hope that there shall be more peace in the world, like in an international school, through globalization and more cross-cultural under-standing.

'Do not do to others
what angers you if done
to you by others.'

Socrates

3

Broken Heart
(By Kasrah, 12 years Old)

Let me tell you that I have two wounds in my heart.

The first wound was inflicted when I was laughed at and taunted by kids at school. They were saying that because I liked a girl, which disgusted them. "What is wrong with liking somebody? Why do those boys say nasty words about me just for having feelings for someone?" This teasing went on for some time until it became unbearable. Whenever my feelings were hurt, I always went to my teacher and confided in her. I always felt better afterwards and went back to studying.

The second wound was caused by kids around me who make fun of my physical features since I have grown so much in the last few months. I am a non-Japanese person attending a Japanese public elementary school.

I have been bullied from the start of grade one, and I have never had a single friend until now, in the sixth grade. I was picked on by a group of 25 boys. This mocking and isolation has left a big scar in my heart. They called me names, and it was especially hard to take when they called me "hairy" because there was nothing I could do about it. I even thought of not going to school anymore. I have been advised by adults to disregard their taunting. I was told that I should ignore them when they say hurtful things because it is normal to have physical changes in your body.

When I couldn't take it anymore, I again told my teacher about it. She talked with those classmates and made them understand how their actions hurt my feelings. Since then they stopped commenting rudely about my appearance, and I now can enjoy school life better.

My dream for the future is to be an architect who can help refugees, people living in poverty, and people with disabilities.

What I want to say here is that no one should keep their worries to themselves. You always have your family, teachers, and friends who care about you and will be there for you. You can go and talk to them and they will always support you.

"Even when terrible things happen to you, go for it!! Never give up!!"

'An eye for an eye
makes the whole world
blind.'

Mahatma Gandhi

My US Experience
(By Mao, 14 years old)

Hello guys!!

I am very satisfied with all the things I've got in my life. I realize how special my life is when I reflect upon previous experiences including living in United States twice in my lifetime. Living there gave me tons and tons of significant experiences. I myself enjoy sharing what I've gained there with my friends, including those that have similar backgrounds. However, my second stay in the US was not all about happiness. I faced a number of ordeals that I realized will never be solved. However, because I worked continuously in coping with all the trials I encountered, happiness overcame the hardships. Now that my problems turned out to have great results, I think that those experiences were inevitable for me to be able to create one of the finest memories in my lifetime. Overall, I learned that the more you work and the harder you try to manage your problems, the greater your success and happiness afterwards.

My story began when I was just nine. I moved to Chicago, USA, which was a totally different environment from that of Japan, where I am originally from. The only thing I could do was hope that I could adapt to this new environment and have lots of friends to play with. As the school year started, I found myself gradually getting used to these new circumstances. I felt very relieved when I had so many friends around me who were very friendly which was more than I expected at first. They would ask me stuff like: Where did you come from? Do you like any sports? Whenever I achieved something big, they would say, "Nice job, Mao!" After a month or so, I joined a soccer team, which was my best team ever. Even now I still can't help wondering how my friends are doing on that team. I felt like I was on top of the world when I was with them. I wasn't alone anymore. Playing soccer abroad and creating relationships by enjoying soccer was my long-term goal. (Actually, I still dream of that.) I saw how that dream isn't impossible to achieve at all.

Nonetheless, my sense of isolation gradually grew in my mind. One day, I was invited to my friend's birthday party. He had been one of the few friends I could really rely on at that time. Since I was proud of being invited to his birthday party, I celebrated from the bottom of my heart. During that day, we started playing dodge ball. I was so afraid of the members picking a game that I didn't know, but this time, I was relieved to hear that we would play dodge ball, a game I knew from Japan. I was so excited that I never realized how other people were playing the game, nor did I try to look at the circumstances until the ball I threw was caught by one of the members whom I didn't really know. It was kind of monumental because of what he said to me then. He said, "I caught the ball!" I turned back and frowned. I couldn't go up to him and say anything. I just kept on gesturing to him and trying to ask him what I was supposed to do after, that but because my English ability wasn't that good at the time, I couldn't. Sadly, however, he just kept on saying the same thing over and over until I was finally told by my benevolent friend that I was supposed to go out from the infield, and that's the American dodge ball rule.

I felt insulted. I was very upset that I didn't have the English skills to cope with this problem. I sort of envied other friends who could say whatever they wanted and interact with ease, and had no trouble getting used to their new environment. On the other hand, I also felt the kindness and generosity that my birthday friend extended to me. I feel this kind of complicated mix of different feelings every time I got in trouble, and it seemed to help me grow in many ways throughout the years I was in America.

Moreover, I was caused great mental stress when I was playing lacrosse at summer camp. The coaches told us to get into groups of two. I didn't know anyone among the players so nobody picked me, and I was left standing alone. The coach finally came up to me and said that there was another guy who didn't have a partner. I went up to him, and we formed a group. I was sort of relieved that there was at least

one other guy that seemed to be looking for a friend as well. As the coach started to tell us what we were going to do after getting into a group of two, he told me, "You are too quiet."

I was frustrated, so I tried my best and said, "What!?"

He told me the same thing again. I knew what he meant but didn't know how to express myself because of my limited language skills. How could I tell them anything if I couldn't explain what I am, who I am, and what I think? I sadly thought that nobody would come up to me or try to be my friend because of my horrible English skills. I felt disappointed in many ways.

Overall, I had an incredible amount of challenges during my stay in the US because of my lack of English skills and uncertainty about how things worked there. However, looking back, I have come to realize how important and necessary those experiences were for me. When I reflect upon those hardships I conclude that they all made me strong. I felt so blessed with many diverse opportunities. Years in the US have given me a bountiful experience and abundant chances to discover new things. I thank all the people who have supported me throughout the years I lived there, including my family and friends.

Thank you for giving me the precious chance to write my story to share with children everywhere.

'Energy and persistence
conquer all things.'

Benjamin Franklin

5

Where Do I Belong?
(By Anna, 14 years old)

When I first heard about this project, and thought about what I could do to help, I got mad. No kidding. When you think about it, why would anyone get mad about helping out other kids? What's wrong with me? I wasn't exactly mad at the project; in fact, I liked the idea. I just couldn't imagine myself participating in any way at first. My first thought was, I can't share anything. I don't have any physical, or for that matter, mental disabilities (well, let's hope not for the mental part). "So what can I say?" But deep inside, I knew that I had troubles. Everybody does. I just didn't want to share them. So now after some consideration, I am writing this story and hoping something will happen.

You are probably wondering what exactly I have in mind when I hear about overcoming difficulties in life. The biggest part of it is just loneliness. It's not like no one talks to me although I went through that kind of phase as well. It's more like I just don't fit in. When your parents are from one country, you live in another, and your school changes again, you're bound to run into trouble. The same goes for me. My first language is Russian, and for a long time it was my best language, though English has probably caught up and passed it. However, I was born in Japan and have lived nowhere else. You can see that this may have interfered a bit in terms of my cultural and ethnic background. This problem relates back to the question that was raised a little while ago for me, "What is your culture?" My first instinctual thought was Russian. But then I think English, since I can't even read and write in Russian. Japanese comes up last even though most of the culture I know is Japanese.

After you read this story you probably think, Ok, that is all cool but what's your problem? Well, loneliness emerges for me when I don't fit in anywhere. Imagine if I talk to Russian kids my age. Although I know the language, I have no idea how they communicate in that society, such as what music they listen to and so on. If I talk to kids from America, there is a similar problem. I do know a huge part of their interests, but I have never lived in the US. Though I live in Japan, I am not fully into their culture. Everywhere I go, I am always a foreigner, even in my native country.

There is no complete solution to this problem. Some people laugh at me when I'm different. Some people want to bully me. Some people pretend I am not there because they find it awkward to talk to me. This is why I have been to so many schools and couldn't stand any of them. However, I have realized the best solution is to ignore them and not let them know that you have been hurt. It is also better to find one community where you won't be pointed at and stared at every time you pass by, and just try to take in their standards. I remember when I was a little kid. I used to think everyone was my friend. I used to get so excited when some Japanese kid down the block invited me to play with them. I would especially get jumping when I met another gaijin (Japanese for foreigner) and thought they would automatically be as excited as I was. But the world doesn't work that way.

When I was five, my parents sent me to the International School in Hokkaido. (Hokkaido was where I was born and where I lived until I was 12). This seemed to be the best option because Japanese Kindergarten would probably give me an even worse start. After a while, I told my mom that it would be better to die than go to a place where no one talks to you. I wasn't the happiest kid on Earth in that school, and that's for sure.

But after the second grade, my parents didn't have enough money for the school and sent me to the Japanese school near our house. The kids liked me for the first week. After their natural curiosity was gone, it was as if I didn't exist most of the time, and sometimes I was an annoying brat that wanted to hang out with them, and cried when they didn't let me. In the summer of that year, I was so depressed, I literally started going crazy. I felt so full of depression at one point that I started throwing up every day, and it was almost impossible to stop me in my mental breakdowns.

This lasted for two weeks, and I started getting back to normal when my parents sent me back to the International School the next year. I didn't really fit in there much better than the first time, but compared to what I just went through, it was much better.

After trying home-schooling and switching schools two more times, I realized it was a waste of effort to try to fit in like I did. I tried to be friends with everybody and didn't realize how different I was. I thought it was my fault that I was a freak, but the kids just couldn't accept me. They didn't even know how, because they had never even seen a foreigner before. I realize now that the only way to cope is to ignore. Not every person in the world is my friend, and they shouldn't be. I shouldn't search for people who are willing to accept me, and it is not my fault I never find them. Crying and going crazy because of people like that is not going to help me either. All I have to do is live my life like it is, and eventually I'll find people who aren't afraid of someone who looks and thinks differently than they do.

'It takes courage to
grow up and become
who you really are.'

E.E. Cummings

6

Living as a Minority in Japan
(By Yeongsu, 14 years old)

I'd like to talk about my nationality, the challenges I faced, and how I overcame these.

Let me start by talking about my nationality. Even though I was born in Japan and have lived here all my life, I'm actually a Korean. Yes, I'm one of the so-called "Zainichi-kankoku jin (Korean-Japanese)." I never went to Korean school nor did I learn Korean at home, so I can't speak Korean well. I might be slightly better at speaking it than Japanese people, though.

Until I graduated elementary school I used the name "Ohta Eiju," not Yeongsu Chang. Why? It was an alias. It's a Japanese-style name tailored for those people of foreign nationality to make living here easier without fear of discrimination. Some time ago, there was a lot of animosity against Korean people in Japan. My Grandpa and Grandma told me so.

Despite this prejudice, I discarded my Japanese name, Ohta Eiju when I enrolled in junior high school. I wanted to live using my real name. I don't know if you understand, but I thought that living as my real self was a very important matter. Even though I've been in Japan since I was born, I always knew I have Korean blood, and I am proud of it. Changing my family name made me slightly embarrassed and uncomfortable, but I don't regret what I've done. Instead, I feel like I was set free! It's already been a year and half and I guess there is no more awkwardness among my classmates, which was always present between my elementary school friends and me. They looked pretty shocked at the junior high school entrance ceremony though. What I feel so deeply now after changing my name is my patriotic spirit for Korea, my home country. Living as a Korean-Japanese, a minority in Japan, without hiding it means having responsibility as a Korean. I believe that I have the opportunity to gain experiences that Koreans who were born and raised in Korea would never have.

This summer I participated in a 7-day study tour to Korea with some 100 Korean-Japanese junior and high school students from all over Japan. All of them live as minorities in Japan, just like me. I made many friends and we still keep in touch via email. We even see each other occasionally. Of course I do have a strong bond with school friends through study and club activities, but there was another kind of bond with my Korean friends! I felt a special connection among us

because of our ethnic background. I think if I were born Japanese here, I would never feel this way.

During my stay in Korea, I had a chance to stay with a local family, the family of a Korean high school student named Da Hae. She is a great painter. Since my Korean conversational skills were not good enough, we spoke in English. I have never lived overseas before and my English is not that good either, but it was then that I realized that English is a very important language to connect people. Without knowledge of Korean, my only communication tool while I was staying in her home was English. I knew my English grammar was terrible, but I tried to keep on speaking to her. Then, a wonderful thing happened. We gradually started being able to understand each other and tell each other everything we were thinking! I was so happy! Although I was so nervous at first, the family was very kind and we made many great memories together. Among those are eating out at a Korean Barbeque restaurant with Da Hae's family, shopping together in Myeong-dong and many more. After I came back to Japan, she sent me an email that really touched me. It went like this:

"The only thing we should always keep is our passionate feeling of sharing the same ethnic blood."

This message was the first time I truly felt that I was one of them. She taught me, a person who wasn't able to speak Korean, that I was a Korean. That was the most important thing to know as a Korean, and I'm really thankful to her for making me realize that. I live on as a Korean now and forever.

In conclusion, I would like to ask something from Japanese people:

Please don't judge us, people of foreign nationality, by biased thoughts or stereotypes. Please stop saying things like "Koreans are always ...." So far, I've never experienced this personally, but I can tell that there are so many adults who have partial views about foreigners. Japan can make the first step towards being a generous country and open its doors to the whole wide world if only adults would be free of their prejudiced views regarding non-Japanese people.

'Nothing is predes-
tined: The obstacles of
your past can become
the gateways that lead
to new beginnings.'

Ralph Blum

7

Together Forever
(By Robert, 15 years old)

I lived in Manila for ten years with my mother and my little sister in an ordinary village. We had a typically big house with three floors to live in. The good thing about it was that we could invite guests like friends and relatives to sleep over in our house so that we could hang out the next day. I usually spent most of my time with my cousins by playing video games, sports, and goofing around. We even used to have a small group of four members: Two of my cousins, my sister, and me. One of my cousins is older than me by two years which made him the leader of the group. However, I think that I was the true leader because I was the one who always gave perfect ideas and decisions. Due to the nature of our competitive relationship, it was natural that we always had arguments on who would be the leader. Even though we fought a lot, we still had a strong bond of friendship between us, and we are also relatives after all. My other cousin, who is the youngest member of the group, liked to be with me most of the time. He asked me a lot of questions or begged me to demonstrate some cool tricks in sports. My little sister always acted as the "peace maker" of our group. She usually did her job when my older cousin and I started a fight; she was always the one who stopped our senseless wars.

We used to meet twice a month because of our school schedules. When we got together outside, we used to go to the malls. Then we decided where to eat before checking out stores. I always preferred to eat in an Italian restaurant since I love to eat pasta and pizza, while the others wanted to eat in a Chinese or Western style restaurant. After a meal, we then went to shops and looked around. I used to go to sports shops since I love sports so much. Because my cousins are video game nerds, they usually wanted to go to game shops or hang out in an arcade center. My sister was the only girl of our group, so she just tagged along wherever we went. We also went to parks so that we could run around a bit. We usually played tag, which was one of my favorite childhood games. I was the fastest runner of our group.

When it came to sports like basketball and soccer, I was the one who was always ready to play and get sweaty. I wasn't really good when it came to studying, but my oldest cousin used to tutor me. He was nice and smart. My other cousin was also a good student, but he wasn't really into arts and music which my sister was good at. She used to play the piano and the recorder. My older cousin could also play the recorder, piano, xylophone and more. I didn't really pay attention to music, but still I used to play the guitar. We thought that we had an amazing and talented group.

After those joyful days, a decision was made by my mother that we will be moving to Tokyo because of my father's work there. My mother wanted a complete family; Mom, Dad, little sister, and myself. When I heard her decision, I tried to mask my disappointment with a forced smile on my face. I complained a lot and asked why we have to move to Japan. It was really hard to break the news to my friends at school and especially to my cousins. They were shocked to know that we had to leave the country, and it made them very sad.

On the day that we had to leave Manila, it was really hard for me to say good-bye to my friends, especially my cousins. I promised them that we would return back to the Philippines during our new school holidays. When we were on the plane, I kept thinking of my friends and cousins that I left behind, and it made me cry a bit.

When we touched down in the land of the rising sun, Japan, we met our father who was waiting for us in the arrival section of the airport. It took us two hours to get to our new house. I was pleased and a bit excited to see our Tokyo home, but it also reminded me of our old house in Manila.

On the first days in my new school, I was really shy when meeting my new school mates. I had a difficult time everyday and didn't know how to talk to them because they were all from different countries. My new school was an international school where students who were raised in different countries study. After around twenty days of attending my

current school, I was able to communicate more with my classmates,and started to feel comfortable.

After a month, I soon realized that I wasn't thinking about my old life in Manila anymore, and was now thinking about my new goals for my fresh start in Japan. My family went back to the Philippines during winter and summer vacations for two weeks to see our friends and relatives. We realized that our group is still as united as ever even if we live far away from each other. It dawned on me that our relationship remained unaffected even if we were miles away from each other.

'Change your thoughts and you change your world.'

Norman Vincent Peale

Teacher Trouble
(By Manya, 12 years old)

It all started a couple years ago when my friend and I joined my previous school. As I was younger, my friend did not care about who she was talking to and loved to interact with everyone. However, I was not the same. I was very shy and preferred to be by myself. This was only the beginning of the year so I had gotten used to my classmates but not the teachers. When a teacher would ask me a question, I would nod or shake my head as a response. At times when I did not understand something, I would be too scared to ask and usually get the work wrong. Once when my friend asked me why I was so scared of them (teachers), I said "Teachers make me feel uncomfortable and sometimes I feel like they don't like me and are against me."

But as the year went on, the teachers would call all the students individually to ask if they had any difficulties with homework or other things that they could help us with. When this happened I would ask my friend questions like, "What are they going to ask me?!" or "What should I say if they say this..."

After almost half a year, I noticed that I was trying to find a way to communicate with teachers without freaking out. I also noticed that I was taking small steps to overcome my fear. The first thing I realized was that when in class a teacher asked me a question I would try to replay with the most detail as possible. Then I noticed that I was starting to take confidence in myself and tell the teachers what was really bothering me. Finally, I noticed that I started asking questions and started to have real conversations. This change helped me in many ways. My class work becoming much better; I understood what was happening in class better and got a lot of praise from the teachers.

Now after many years and lots of progress, I can interact with teachers a lot better and am now one of the loudest and most cheerful people in the whole class.

'Nothing in life is to be feared. It is only to be understood.'

Marie Curie

9

My Fear of Public Speaking
(By JJ, 12 years old)

From the time I was little, I have had trouble talking in front of a group of people. I really enjoy writing speeches, planning presentations and doing other things like that. Still, I freeze up when I start talking and start to lose my confidence. I have tried to overcome my fear, but it's not as easy as it seems. You can't control the way you feel or act; it just comes naturally, and for me the biggest reason why I hate having this fear, is that it affects my presentation. No matter how great the speech is, the message doesn't get to the audience.

It might seem like it isn't a big deal, but this problem prevents me from doing many things, even performing something for a concert or something out of school. When I was younger, it wasn't such a big problem because there weren't many serious presentations that would be graded or be watched by as many people. I was thus able to forget about this problem for a while.

This year, I started having many major assessment tasks that involved me talking in front of the class. When I first heard about these presentations, I started to panic and when the day comes that I have to present, I get really nervous even if I practice a lot.

On the last project we had to do, I needed to talk in front of the entire class and do a speech. I was really nervous because it was one of the important requirements for the task, and the teacher would be marking me. I was trembling when he called my name to do the presentation. I memorized all the words to my speech and knew exactly what to do, so I wondered why I was so nervous.

To my surprise, when I got up there, I didn't feel even slightly nervous. The speech felt like a breeze, and I knew that I had done a good job. My teacher told me that I had great confidence during the speech, and I was shocked because I didn't know that I did it that well.

After this experience, I haven't been as nervous as other times because now I can control myself and make sure not to do anything wrong. I am proud of myself for overcoming my fear. Even now, I'm not jumping with joy when I have to do a speech, but I'm not trembling with fear either.

'Life shrinks or
expands in proportion
to one's courage.'

Anais Nin

About the Charity Organization Gawad Kalinga:

Gawad Kalinga began with a youth camp taking in 127 juvenile delinquents who were former gang members in Bagong Silang, Caloocan City. From 1996 to 1999, social engineering began; bringing education and training for gang members, and the first GK house was built for a family. In 2000, Gawad Kalinga finally launched; a few programs such as shelter were started, signaling the start of an organization that would eventually be stationed in 8 different 'GK countries'.

'Gawad Kalinga is now being implemented in almost 1,700 communities in the Philippines and in other developing countries such as Indonesia, Cambodia and Papua New Guinea. It has become a concrete manifestation of the healing of relationships in the Philippines, bridging the gap between the rich and the poor, government and the private sector by simply "bayanihan," the willing sharing of any heavy load for the good of his fellowmen. Driven by a strong commitment to faith, GK is able to bring out the patriotism in every Filipino by making him a hero to his country – a "bayani" that can contribute to "bagong bahay, bagong buhay, bagong bayan

(new home, new life, new country)." At a time when most are happy to leave the country to look for greener pastures, Gawad Kalinga sparks hope in the Filipino dream – to restore this great nation and once again be proud to be Filipino.' (gk1world.com)

The founder of Gawad Kalinga is Antonio Meloto, known as Tito (meaning Uncle) Tony, born on January 17, 1950. *'At a young age, he was already exposed to the squalid living conditions of the poor, his home being near a shoreline squatter community where poverty was already very pronounced, even in the 1950s.'* (gk1world.com) In 1995, he was inspired to start a youth program in Bagong Silang, leading to the formation of the organization known as Gawad Kalinga.

This organization exists for the purpose of improving the lives of children and adults alike, one way being through the GK Child and Youth Development Program, which provides infrastructure, values formation programs, and constructive activities for disadvantaged children in GK sites.

This is one of the reasons why the author chose this organization; it benefits people who live in poverty who survive without adequate resources, many of them adolescents like me. They give young people another chance at life.

*All profits made in selling this book will go to Gawad Kalinga's youth projects, which will help give a better quality of life for people in the GK communities.

転んで、学んで、
立ち上がる

アリヨ・ハーディ

転んで、学んで、立ち上がる

はじめに

この本を選んでくださった読者のみなさんに、著者から御礼申し上げます。選んでくださった理由が、日本での実生活の中で若者たちが抱える問題への興味だったにしろ、著者が行なうチャリティープロジェクトを支援してくださるためだったにしろ、この本を読んでいただくことがみなさんにとって有意義なこととなることを心から願っています。

　人生において、私たちは皆、打ちひしがれたり逃げ出したくなるような困難を経験します。そして時には、本当にあきらめてしまう時だってあります。でも、同じあきらめるにしても、自分ができることのすべてを出し切って、というのがやはり一番です。また、困難を乗り越え、勝利を勝ち取るときもあります。その勝利の喜びは格別です！それが、ちょうどみなさんと同世代の若者たちが実際に困難にぶつかり全力で立ち向かった経験談を分かち合いたいと思うきっかけでした。彼らは転んでも、必ずもう一度立ち上がって日々乗り越える努力をし続け、そして今日の勝利をつかんでいるのです。

　この本は車のようなもの、そして綴られている言葉は窓のようなものです。みなさんはこれらで他の人たちの人生を垣間見ることができるわけです。ありとあらゆる困難は誰にでもふりかかるものです。様々な人生の中をドライブすることで、みなさんが自分自身の抱えている問題や困難を解決する糸口を見出していただけたら、と願っています。すべてのストーリーは日本に住んでいる

様々な国籍の若者たちによって書かれたものです。彼らは、それぞれの困難に独自の方法で立ち向かい、乗り越えてきたのです。

たとえその困難が朝起きるのもイヤになるほどうんざりするようなものだったとしても、全力で立ち向かえば後悔はないのです。本当に。

謝辞

　　多くの人たちの様々な支えや協力がなければ、この本を完成させることができませんでした。まず誰よりも最初に感謝したいのは、どんなときでも僕を信じてくれている両親です。母は出版社や慈善団体との段取りをしてくれました。母の協力には本当に感謝しています。母なしにはこの本を作り上げることができませんでした。また、いつもあたたかい愛情をもって支えてくれる父にも感謝しています。父からこの本を作ろうというインスピレーションを受けました。このプロジェクトを指導し、多くの素晴らしいアイデアをくれた、私の担任であるノエル・サウソール先生にも心から感謝しています。先生の支えとご意見は本を書き上げる様々な過程において大きな助けとなりました。また、特にお礼を申し上げたいのは、中学校長のシュナイダー先生です。今回のプロジェクト実現に向けて、承認してくださり、学校関係者のみなさんへのお知らせなどを発信してくださいました。私の英語の先生であるクッセン先生も、クラスのみんなにこの本のためにそれぞれがもつ実話を寄稿することを奨励してくれました。本当に感謝しています。

　　そして、本書のために寄稿してくれたすべての私の友人たちに感謝します。自分の弱みを世界中の人々の前にさらけ出すということは非常に難しいことです。彼らは私のプロジェクトをより素晴らしいものにすべく手をかしてくれました。彼らの勇気と誰かを助けたいと

いう気持ちを心からほめたたえたいと思います。

　　また、本書すべてを日本語に翻訳してくれた大河内博美さんにも心から感謝申し上げます。多くの作業にも気長に取り組んでくれて、本当にありがたいと思っています。

　　最後に、この本を買ってくださった皆さんには感謝してもしきれないほどです。こうして誰かの生活を少しでもよくすることができるということは、私にとってこのうえなく意味のあることなのです。もし誰か困難を抱えている人をご存知でしたら、ぜひこの本のことを話してさし上げてください。

‘失敗はつらいが、成功
のための努力をしない
よりずっとましだ。’

セオドア・ルーズベルト

1

アレルギー発作
アリヨ（15歳）

　すべては僕が生後4カ月のときに始まった。ひどいぜんそく症状を起こし始めたのだ。それはどんどん悪化し、3歳になるまでのほとんどを病院で過ごすことになった。常に薬づけの日々。通っていた幼稚園もほとんど毎日欠席という状態だった。さらに小学校にあがるころから、多くの種類の食べ物にひどいアレルギー反応を起こすようになってしまった。

　まず、僕はほとんどのお菓子を食べることができなかった。上白糖が含まれているからだ。いわゆるジャンク・フードの類も、それに含まれている食用油、脂肪、添加物のせいで食べることができなかった。イーストと小麦もダメだったので、ほとんどの種類のパンも食べることができなかったし、冷たい食べ物は吐き気をもよお

すので食べられなかった。牛乳も米も、他にもたくさん食べられないものがあった。最悪の相性だったのは卵だった。ただでさえ食べられない食べ物をあげればキリがないほどの僕だったのに、卵ときたら、それはそれは多くの食べ物に含まれている原材料だ。食べられるものの方が食べられないものの数よりずっと少なかったんだ！クラスの中で僕だけが普通の食べ物を食べられないなんて不公平だと感じていた。遠足の時もバースディパーティーに呼ばれたときも、母が作ってくれたアレルゲン・フリーのランチボックスを持っていき、他の子どもたちが食べているおいしそうな食べ物を横目に見ながらそれを食べなければならなかった。

5年生になったとき、アレルギーのせいで僕の身体はすっかり衰弱し、長い間学校にも行けなくなってしまった。ほとんどの時間を、家のリビングのソファーで、母が作ってくれる味気のない『アレルギー食』を食べながら過ごした。それでも、文句は言えなかった。なぜなら、もしも口にしちゃいけないものを食べたり飲んだりしてしまったら、ひどいアレルギー反応を引き起こして、容赦なく襲ってくる激しいかゆみと高熱に苦しむことになるからだ。それだけじゃない。太陽の下で遊ぶこともできなかった。陽に当たると、肌が服に触れただけでも火がついたように痛みが走るほどの発疹が出たからだ。皮膚が治る過程でも、眠っているときでさえどうしてもかゆくて掻きむしってしまうため、僕の顔も身体もピンクから赤のグラデーションで覆われてしまっていた。僕

を見る人々の視線がいつもつらかった。毎日毎日悲しい思いで、こんなことが初めから起こらなければよかったのにと願っていた。普通の子どものようになったり、治ったりすることなんてありえないと思っていたから。僕の両親は定期的にお医者さんに連れて行って、一体何が悪いのか知ろうとしたけれど、結果はいつも同じではっきりしなかった。ただ、さらにたくさん薬を出されるだけ。

　　　毎日、体力的にも精神的にもぐったりしていた。両親の目にもどうやら治療がうまくいってないと映ったようで、思い切って治療方法を変えることになった。最初の大きな第一歩は、僕の生活スタイル全部を完全にリセットすることだった。食事、睡眠、運動にいたるまですべてだ。食べてもいいとわかっているものだけを食べ、その他の食べ物は完全に排除した。また、それまで処方されていたアレルギー薬やステロイドの常用がかえって僕の健康を害していたため、それらの使用をすっぱりやめた。皮膚を覆うひどい発疹やとめどなく爪でひっかいてできた赤い傷を隠すためにクリームを使っていたけれど、このクリームは単に傷を隠すだけのもので治すものではなかった。このクリームの使用をやめた当初、僕の皮膚は赤みがすごく増し、またかゆくなったけれど、そのうち良くなってきた。マクロバイオティックの食事療法士、カイロプラクティック療法士、そして僕のために自然療法を学んでくれた母が、僕が食べられる食べ物を

転んで、学んで、立ち上がる

少しずつ増やし、身体のバランスを取り戻し、システムをもう一度構築しなおして新しくやり直すことができるように手助けしてくれた。とても長い道のりだったし、途中にはいい時も悪い時もたくさんあった。目覚めたときに、初めて夜じゅうぐっすり眠ったと実感できた朝のことを、僕は今でもはっきりと思い出せる。誰の助けもいらずベッドから飛び出して、階段を駆け下りて家族に「おはよう！」と言えたんだ。これが、僕が良くなっていると初めて実感できた時だったのだと思う。まるで毎日じわじわと笑いがこみ上げてきて、もう自分でも止められないって思うくらいまでその笑顔がどんどん大きくふくらんでくるような感じだった。

　　学校に登校できる日も増えていき、お天気の日でも外で遊べるようになり、夜もぐっすり眠れるようになっただけでなく、ずっと長い間食べられなかった食べ物も食べられるようになった。3年かかって、ついに僕は完全に良くなって、自分がしたいことをなんでもできる可能性がいっぱいの明るい将来を見つめることができるようになったんだ。ボールのようにまんまるく縮こまって何もかも投げ出したいほどつらい時もたくさんあったけれど、どんな時でも僕の家族と友達が応援してくれた。彼らこそが、今の僕へと導いてくれたんだと思う。あのつらい日々を僕は絶対に忘れることはないけれど、でもその分、僕をここまで導いてくれた愛すべき人々がいることが僕の人生の財産になった。どんなときも僕のことを信じてくれた両親へのこの恩は一生かかっても返せな

いほどだ。母は一日たりと怠ることなく、僕のために尽くしてくれた。父は忙しくてやらなければならないことも山積みだったのにもかかわらず、仕事から帰ると僕の世話をする家族を一所懸命手伝ってくれた。両親は夜も交替で僕の番をしてくれ、母は僕をどうにかして良くしようと四方八方手を尽くして調べてくれた。父は衰弱して歩くことさえできなかった僕を背負ってトイレに連れて行ってくれたり、家の中を移動させてくれたりした。特に僕が落ち込んだときには二人ともなぐさめてくれた。妹は自分の食事のときに僕がうらやましがって悲しい思いをしないようにとわざわざキッチンに隠れて食べてくれていた。

　　試練を乗り越えた今となっては、アレルギーの日々の一番つらかった時というのを思い出せない。僕の人生のなかでも最悪だった5年生のあの数ヶ月間はぽっかりと記憶に穴があいてしまったかのように抜け落ちてしまっているんだ。多分、それは僕が小さい頃のままに正気を保てるように僕の記憶中枢がうまく守ってくれるように働いているんだと思う。後で、このことを調べてみたら、どうやら軽度の解離性健忘であるようだとわかった。これは精神的に痛手となるような非常に衝撃的な経験をした場合にそれを記憶の奥にしまいこもうとするときにおこるものだ。だからといって僕が小さい頃のことを何も覚えていないということじゃなく、ただ、具合が悪かった間のことがほとんど思い出せないっていうことなんだ。僕が良くなってから、両親が当時のことを

色々話してくれるけれど、それでもまだ思い出せないこともある。

　　この経験のあと、僕の人生はまっさらの状態になった。人生をもう一度やり直すチャンスをもらったんだ。僕はそのチャンスを受け取り、そして今ここで、大きな夢を持つ普通の子どもとして生きている。今は何でも食べたいものを食べ、身体だってまるでアレルギーなんかなかったかのように好調だ。この試練に向き合ったことで僕は強くなった。そして命を大事に思うこと、自分の中に秘められた力を信じることの大切さを学んだ。だからこそ、今、目標に向かってがんばっていたり、何らかの障害を乗り越えようとしたりしているすべての人々の幸運を祈っている。僕のこの経験談が、みんながどんなことにも全力を尽くすことにつながるように願ってやまない。

転んで、学んで、立ち上がる

'世界は苦難に満ち
ている。また、それ
を乗り越えることに
も満ちている。'

ヘレン・ケラー

2

すべては文化のせいで…
チィンテン（14歳）

　　それはいつものような曇りの日の英語の授業。クラスメートと私は席についてノートをとり、教科書を読み、いろいろなことについて話し合っていた。ところが、今日の授業にかぎって、先生は『第三文化の子どもたち』という題のプリント綴りを私たちに読ませると言った。

　　私は内心、「第三文化の子どもたち、それって私のような子どものことじゃないか、私の過去、現在、そして未来のことじゃ？」と思った。そして、その文書を読み進むにつれ、前の学校での数々の出来事がまるで数日前のことのようによみがえってきた。それはすべて、私の文化のせいで起こったことだった。

74

　まず最初に、私のことを少し知ってほしい。実は私はここ日本の東京で生まれた。けれど、私の両親は中国上海の出身だ。だから1歳のころ、中国に渡ってそれから8年間中国の祖父母と暮らした。

　2005年に東京に戻ってきたけれど、もうまったく昔いたころの記憶はなく、単によその知らない町という感じだった。何より、自分の国籍が日本人であるということすら知らなかったし、その当時の両親がどんな風だったのかも知らなかった。数ヵ月後、なんとか少し日本語も学んで学校に入った。そこですべては起こった。

　すべては、私が5年生で初めて通った学校に転入したときに始まった。そこはインターナショナル・スクールだったので、日本人でない生徒も多いだろうと思っていた。たしかに、日本人は少なかったけれど、一番人数の多い外国人派閥になっていたのは韓国人生徒たちだった。私はそれまで韓国人と知り合ったことがなかったので、当初は彼らと知り合えて、一緒に勉強したり遊んだりできて、とてもうれしく思っていた。ところが、そのうちに状況は変わってしまった。スンイルという少年が私の前に現れ、このときに私と韓国人生徒たちの間に衝突の種が芽生え始めたのだった。

　スンイルは、目が小さくて鼻がとがった巻き毛の背の低い韓国人少年だった。どういうわけか、彼が誰かと遊んでいる様子はちょっとかわいらしく、とても活発

で陽気な子だった。ある日、私が毎朝他の生徒たちにするのと同じように彼に挨拶しようとすると、彼はちらりと私を見たきり、向こうをむいてしまった。それで、私もカチンときたけれども、深呼吸して自分を抑えた。「たぶん彼はシャイすぎるんだ。」と自分に言い聞かせた。彼だって、私と同じその年に入ってきた転入生だったのだから。「まぁ、そのうち仲良くなれるだろう。」でも、そんな日は訪れなかった。

　学校生活がすすむにつれ、徐々にスンイルがちょっとイヤなことをすることに気づきはじめた。ある時は唐突に私の鼻をつついて、さっと逃げていったりした。最初はただふざけてからかっているのかと思ったので気にしていなかったのだが、だんだん度が過ぎてきた。最後にはスンイルは大胆にも私の気付かないときに耳につばを吐きかけてきたり、僕が一人でいるときに韓国人の友達を呼び寄せて階段から突き落としたりした。ある日、本当にスンイルのことが気になったので昼休みに彼のところへ行ってみた。担任の先生はどこかに行っていていなかった。

　「ねぇ、スンイル。」私は少し顔をしかめながら言った。「聞きたいことがあるんだけど。」

　彼はゆっくり僕を見上げ、5秒間くらいじっと見ていた。そして、それから、彼の眼は見開かれ、言葉がまるで台風が吹きつけるように飛び出してきた。

転んで、学んで、立ち上がる

「俺の目の前からうせろ！中国人はみんな豚だ！」

　　私はびっくりし、何人かのクラスメートは何事かとこっちをみた。スンイルと他の韓国人少年たちに教室から押し出される前に「何？」というのがやっとだった。彼らはみんな私より背が低かったし、彼らがまとめてかかってきても私の方が強いということもわかっていたけれど、私は何もせず、ただ教室のドアを目の前でぴしゃりと閉めさせるままにしたのだった。私にはわからなかった。なぜ、理由もなく彼らはあんなことをしてくるのだろう。その時はそれしか考えられなかった。ドアを見つめながら頭はからっぽになった。こんなことは初めてのことで、しかも突然のあっという間の出来事だったから。自分でも気付かないうちに、私の頬を涙がつたい、足元のカーペットに落ちてにじんでいった。

　　その日、母にそのことを話すと、母はひどく怒って苛立った。すぐにペンと紙を持ってきて学校の事務局あての手紙を書き始めた。その時に私が思っていたのは、とにかくこんなことが起こったなんて信じたくないということだけで、これがもっと大きな騒動の始まりだったとは知る由もなかった。

　　学校事務局は母からの手紙を受け取ると、当時の担任の先生に注意喚起するように連絡をし、きちんと解決するように指示した。手紙が事務局に届いたその日の

78

お昼休みに先生はクラス全員を集めて私の今回の出来事について話した。彼は、スンイルのしたことは中国人に対する差別で、してはならないひどいことだと言ったが、スンイルは先生に反論し、彼が私にしたことを正当化する多くの理由を述べたてた。さらに、韓国人生徒たち全員、前は私と仲良くしてくれていた生徒までもが立ち上がり、先生を指差し、スンイルの言ったことを支持することを怒鳴りだしたのだ。過去にあった中国人との小さないさかいのことに始まり、第二次世界大戦で中国が南北に分かれた朝鮮において韓国を相手に戦ったことにいたるまで。その言い争いの声量もすさまじく、言い表せないほどで、校長先生さえ、一体何事かと教室までくるほどだった。彼が韓国人生徒たちをなだめ、彼らに中国人と韓国人に関することをたくさん話してくれた。校長先生の前でもまだ反論する生徒も何人かいたが、最後には全員静かになった。私はこの騒動の間中、一言も口をきかず、ただ目に浮かんだ涙をとどめるのが精いっぱいだった。それから校長先生はインターナショナル・スクールの方針について話し、それにより世界中の子どもを受け入れること、中国人の子どもであっても例外ではないと言った。また、校長先生は韓国人生徒たちに、韓国人と中国人は仲良くなるべきで、このような騒動は二度と起こってはいけないと話した。校長先生が教室を去ると、私はほっと胸をなでおろし、教室の中では長い沈黙が続いた。

　数日後、私とスンイル、それぞれの両親は、皆学校の事務局に呼ばれ、事務局長、校長先生、担任の先生

と一連の騒動について話し合うことになった。話し合いの間、やっと自分に力を取り戻し、どのようにスンイルが自分にひどい仕打ちをしたのか、どのように「騒動」が始まったのか、皆に説明をした。すぐに、スンイルは私の顔を指差して反論してきたけれど、すぐに彼の母親に止められ、その後は話し合いの間中沈黙していた。ただひたすら私をにらみつけていただけだ。話し合いの1週間後、スンイルは退学になった。スンイルが退学になった翌日、教室の韓国人生徒たちは皆すっかり変わった。彼らは私のことを普通のいい友達として扱い、私は残りの学校生活を幸せに過ごすことができた。

　　プリントを読み終え、私は第三文化の子どもみたいだなと感じた。日本で生まれ、日本国籍も持っているのに、ほとんどの自分の先祖は中国人だと思う。今通っている学校にも何人か韓国人の友達がいるけれど、誰もスンイルのような子ではない。そのことをとてもうれしく思うし、インターナショナル・スクールでそうであるように、グローバリゼーションと相互理解を深めることで世界がもっと平和になるように願っている。

‘他人からされたら怒るようなことを人にしてはいけない。’

ソクラテス

3

心の中にある傷

キャスラ（12 歳）

心の中にある傷を二つ言います。

一つは、学校ですきな女の子がいると言って笑われたり、気持ち悪いと言われたことです。「好きな人がいることの何が悪いの？なぜそのことで男子に暴言を言われたりするの？」もう耐えられなくなるまでしばらくこのいやがらせは続きました。心を傷つけられるときに先生に相談します。そうするとすっきりして元気よく勉強することができるのです。

もう一つは、ここ数カ月でずいぶん成長した身体のことで学校のみんなにあれこれ言われたことです、僕は日本人じゃないけれど公立の小学校に通っています。いじめは小学校１年生のときに始まり、６年生になった今

まで一人も友達がいません。25人の男子グループにいじめられていました。バカにされたり、孤独になったりしたことは、僕の心に大きな傷を残しました。彼らは色々な呼び方をしてきましたが、特にイヤだったのは「毛深い」と言われた時です。だってそれは僕にはどうしようもできないことだからです。もう学校なんかに行きたくないと思うほどでした。大人の人たちからは、そういう中傷は気にしなければいいと言われました。誰の身体でも変わってくるのは当たり前のことなんだから、彼らが嫌なことを繰り返し言い始めても無視しなさいと言われました。

また我慢できなくなると、先生に話しに行きました。先生はそれらの生徒たちに、自分たちのしたことがどれだけ僕のことを傷つけることなのかということを彼らが理解するまで話してくれました。それからは彼らが僕の外見のことでひどいことを言ってくることはなくなり、今では学校生活をずっと楽しめるようになりました。

僕の将来の夢は、難民や貧困にあえぐ人々、また障害をもつ人々の役に立てるような建築家になることです。

僕が言いたいことは、悩みを自分のなかに貯めてはいけないということです。誰にも、いつだって親身になってくれる家族、先生、そして友達がいるはずです。何かあった時は、彼らに話してみてください。きっと力になってくれるはずです。

「どんなにイヤなことがあってもがんばれ！あきらめるな！」

‘「目には目を」という考え方では、世界中の目をつぶしてしまうことになる。’

マハトマ・ガンジー

僕のアメリカ体験
マオ（13歳）

やあ、みんな！！

　　僕は、自分の人生のすべてにおいてとても満足している。生まれてから２回もアメリカで生活する機会があったことを含め、今までの様々な経験を思うにつけ、僕の人生は本当に素晴らしいとしみじみ思う。アメリカでの生活では本当に多くの経験をすることができた。そこで得たことを、同じような経験をしてきた友達だけでなく多くの友人と共有することも楽しんでいる。だけど、僕の２度目のアメリカ生活は楽しいことばかりじゃなかった。絶対に乗り越えられないと思うような困難にもたくさんぶつかった。それでも、すべての問題にあきらめることなく取り組み続けることで最終的には困難を乗り越え、幸せを手にすることができたんだ。今となっては

それらの困難もいい結果となっていて、僕が思うに、それらの経験も僕の人生での最高の思い出を得るのに不可欠だったのに違いない。つまり、自分の問題に対して一所懸命頑張れば頑張るほど、さらに挑戦すればするほど、後で得る成功や喜びはより大きなものになるということを僕は学んだんだ。

　　　僕の話は、僕がちょうど9歳のときに始まる。生まれた日本とは何もかもが違うアメリカのシカゴに引っ越した。とにかく新しい環境になじんでたくさんの友達ができるといいな、と願うのみだった。学校生活が始まると、徐々にその新しい環境になじんでいっているのが自分でもわかった。当初期待していたよりもたくさんの気さくな友達ができたことでも僕はほっとした。彼らは、「どこから来たの？」「スポーツは何が好き？」などと尋ねてきたし、僕がなにかすごいことができたときにはいつでも「すごいよ、マオ！」とほめてくれた。1か月くらいたったころ、サッカーチームに入った。それは僕の中では最高のチームだった。今でも、つい、チームのみんなはどうしてるかなぁなどと考えてしまうくらいだ。彼らと一緒にいると、まるで世界の頂点に立っているような気分だった。もう一人じゃなかった。海外でサッカーをして、サッカーを通じて素晴らしい関係を築くことは、僕たちが共に夢みている将来の目標だった。（実際、僕は今でもそれを夢みている。）この夢がかなわないわけがないと信じていた。

それにもかかわらず、僕の中で少しずつ孤独感が大きくなってきていた。ある日、友達の誕生日パーティーに招待された。彼は、当時僕が本当に頼れる数少ない友人の一人だった。彼がパーティーに呼んでくれたことがとてもうれしかったし、心から彼の誕生日を祝っていた。その日、ドッジボールをすることになった。みんなが僕の知らないゲームを始めようとしたらどうしようと心配していたけれど、日本でもやったこともあり、なじみのあるドッジボールをすると聞いてほっとした。自分が投げたボールが知らない子にキャッチされるまで、みんながどんな風にプレーしているかに気付かなかっただけでなく、周りをみる余裕もなかったことが悔やまれるけれど、その時に彼が僕に放った言葉はなんだかとてつもないようなものに感じた。彼は「ボールをとったぞ！」と言った。僕は戻って顔をしかめた。彼のところに行って何か言うこともできなかった。その時はまだ英語もそこまでよくできなかったので、ただ身振り手振りで、このあと僕はどうすればいいのと彼に聞き続けた。でも悲しいことに、最終的に僕の親切な友達がアメリカのドッジボールのルールでは、僕は内野から出なくちゃいけないんだと教えてくれるまで、彼は同じことを繰り返し言い続けていた。僕はとても侮辱された気分だった。こんなこともうまくやりとりできない自分の英語力のなさが悔しかった。新しい環境になじむ苦労もなく、なんでも言いたいことが言えて、なんでもなくコミュニケーションできるみんながうらやましかった。でも一方で、誕生日パーティーによんでくれた友達の僕への親切や優しさも感じていた。毎回何か問題にぶつかるたびに、僕

はこんな風に色々な感情が入り混じった複雑な気持ちに
なったのだが、それがアメリカでの何年かの生活を通じ
て僕がいろんな意味で成長できたことにつながったよう
に思う。

　さらに、サマーキャンプでのある日、ラクロスを
していた時に起きた出来事は僕に精神的な打撃を与えた。
コーチは僕たちに二人ずつのグループに分かれるように
指示した。その中の誰とも知りあいじゃなかった僕は、
誰からも選んでもらえず、一人とり残されてしまった。
最後にコーチが来てパートナーのいない子がもう一人い
るから、と言った。僕は彼のところへ行き、パートナー
になった。僕以外にも少なくとももう一人友達を探して
いる子がいたというのは、ある意味、ほっとした。二人
ずつに分かれた後にコーチが何をするのか説明しはじめ
たとき、彼がこう言った。「君は静かすぎるよ。」僕は
苛立ちを感じて、精いっぱいがんばって「何だっ
て！？」と言い返した。　すると彼はまた同じことを言
った。彼の意味することは分かっていたけれど、限られ
た英語力で自分をどうやって表現したらいいのかわから
なかった。僕が誰で、どんな人間なのか、何を考えてい
るのかも説明できない状態で、一体何を言えるというの
だろう。自分の英語がこんなんじゃ、もう誰も僕のとこ
ろへ来てくれないし、誰も友達になろうとしてくれない
んじゃないかと悲しい思いにしずんだ。いろんなことに
幻滅を感じていた。

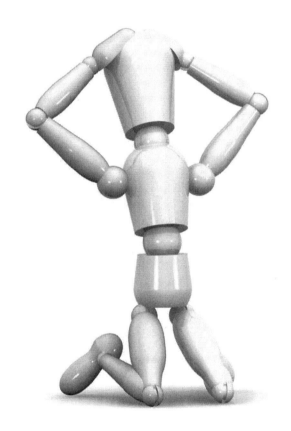

　　英語力もあまりなく、アメリカではどんなふうに物事がすすんでいくのかも知らなかった僕は、アメリカでの生活で本当にたくさんの挑戦をしなければならなかった。でも、振り返ってみると、それらがどれだけ自分にとって大切で必要なことだったか、改めて実感している。

　　自分が経験した困難の数々のことをじっくり考えるにつけ、それらすべてが僕を強くしてくれたんだと思う。色々な機会を与えられたことは本当に恵まれていると思った。アメリカでの生活は、僕に余りある経験と数えきれないほどの新しい発見をするチャンスをくれた。僕のアメリカでの数年間を支えてくれた家族や友達、その他すべての人たちに感謝している。最後に、僕の経験を世界中の子どもたちと分かち合える機会を与えてくれたことに心から感謝したい。

'エネルギーと忍耐
強さがあれば、すべ
てに打ち勝つことが
できる。'

ベンジャミン
フランクリン

5

私は何者？
アンナ（14歳）

　　このプロジェクトの話を初めて聞いて、私に何ができるか考えたとき、怒りが込み上げてきた。冗談じゃなく。どうして孤児を助けるってことで怒りを感じる人間がいると思う？私はどうかしてる？　本当のところ、このプロジェクトに怒りは感じていない、むしろいい考えだと思う。でも、最初、自分がどんなふうにその中で協力していけるのか、想像もつかなかった。とにかく最初に心に浮かんだのは、「分かち合うことなんて何もない」ということだった。身体的にも精神的にもこれといって障害も問題もない（まぁ、精神面は本当に大丈夫であると願うとして）。じゃあ、何が話せる？でも、本当は、私の奥底にはいろんな問題があることをわかっている。きっと、誰もがそうだ。ただ私はそれをみんなと分かち合いたくはないだけだった。ずいぶん色々悩んだけ

94

れど、今、ここに書いてみようと思う。これで何かが起こることを願って。

　　人生での困難を乗り越えるっていうことを聞いたときに私がどんなことを思い浮かべたんだろうってみんなは思っていると思う。その大半は単に孤独だけじゃない。誰も話しかけてくれないとかそんなことじゃない。そういう時期もあったけれど。むしろ、逆に私がなじめないと言った方がしっくりくる。両親が生まれた国と自分が住んでいる国が違って、学校も転校つづき（たくさんの学校に）となると、当然のように問題を抱えることになる。私も例にもれずそうだ。私の第一言語はロシア語で、今では多分英語の方が得意になっているくらいかもしれないけれど、長い間ロシア語が一番得意だった。日本で生まれ、他の国には住んだことがない。そのことが私自身の文化や民族的な部分に何らかの影響を与えていることは誰にでもわかると思う。これが、ずいぶん長い間私の中にある疑問「私の文化は何？」ということに関係してきている。私がとっさに思い浮かべるのは「ロシア文化」、でも、そのあと、「英語の文化」と思い直す。なぜなら、ロシア語では読むことも書くこともできないから。それから自分がいちばん馴染みのある「日本文化」が最後に浮かんでくる。

　　これを読んだ人は、「ふうん、いいじゃない、何が問題なの？」と思うだろう。まず、どこにもなじめないとき、私の中には孤独がわきあがってくる。同い年の

ロシア人の子どもと話す私を想像してみてほしい。言葉を知っていても、その社会の中でどうやってつきあっていっていいのかわからないのだ。たとえば、彼らがどんな音楽を聴いているのかもわからない、等々。アメリカ人の子どもと話すときにも同じような問題が生じる。彼らがどんなことに興味があるのか、大体のことは知っているけれど、実際アメリカに住んだこともないわけだから。そして、また、私は日本に住んではいるけれど日本の文化に完全に溶け込んでいるわけじゃない。どこにいっても、自分の国でですえ、私はいつも「外国人」なのだ。

　　これに完璧な解決方法などない。私が他の人と違うということで、笑う人だっている。いじめようとする人もいる。なんだか私に話しかけるのも居心地が悪く感じて、私の存在すら無視する人もいる。そのせいでたくさんの学校を転々とし、どの学校にもなじむことができなかった。でも、自分なりに一番いい解決方法にたどりついた。それは、彼らを無視すること、自分が傷ついたということを悟られないようにすることだ。自分が指差されたり、毎度通り過ぎるたびに物珍しそうに見られたりしない仲間を見つけて、彼らの基準を受け入れるというのもいい。まだ幼くて誰もが自分の友達だと思っていたころのことを思い出す。その頃は日本人の子どもたちが一緒に遊ぼうとさそいに来てくれるのがとてもうれしかった。特に他の「ガイジン」に出会うと、彼らも当然私と同じようにうれしいであろうと思って、飛び上がっ

て喜んだ。でも世界はそんな風には回っていなかったのだ。

　私が5歳になると、両親は私を北海道にあるインターナショナル・スクールに入れた。（私は北海道で生まれ、12歳まで北海道に住んでいた。）日本の幼稚園に行っていたら、もっと大変なスタートになっただろうから、それが一番いい選択だったのだと思う。しばらくして、母に、誰も話してくれないようなところに通わなくちゃいけないなら死んだ方がましだと言った。本当にその学校での私は不幸だったのだ。

　2年生のあと、両親はその学校の学費が払えなくなり、家の近くの公立学校に私を入れた。最初の週は子どもたちに好かれていた。だが、珍しさからの興味をなくすと、まるで存在がないかのように無視され、しつこくくっついてきては入れてくれないと泣く、面倒な邪魔者扱いをされるようになった。その年の夏、私はずいぶん落ち込んで、文字通り狂い始めていた。すっかりうつ状態になり、毎日吐くようになっていて、何をしても気分がよくなることはなかった。これが2週間ほど続き、翌年、両親がまたインターナショナル・スクールに私を戻すと、普通の状態になおりはじめた。前に通っていたときよりなじめたとは言えないけれど、それでも、公立学校で受けてきた苦しみを思えば、ずっとましだった。

転んで、学んで、立ち上がる

ホーム・スクーリング（自宅学習）やさらに２回の転校を経て、自分がなじもうと努力してきたことは無駄だったのだと悟った。自分がどんなふうにみんなと違うのかもわからないままに、とにかく仲良くなろうとしてきた。自分が変わり者扱いされるのは自分のせいだとずっと思っていたけれど、そうではなく、単に子どもたちが私を受け入れてくれなかっただけだったのだ。外国人をみたことすらなかった彼らは、どうやって受け入れたらいいかわからなかったのだ。

　今は、唯一のやりすごす方法は無視することだとわかった。世界中の人がみな私の友達なわけじゃないし、そうあるべきでもない。自分を受け入れてくれそうなひとを探して歩く必要はないし、見つからなくてもわたしのせいじゃない。受け入れてくれない人たちのせいで泣いたり狂いそうな気持ちになったりするのはひとつも自分の助けにならない、ということもわかった。とにかく私の人生をあるがままに生きること、そうすればやがて、自分と違った外見や考え方をする人間を恐れない人に出会えるだろうと思う。

‘勇気がなければ、
成長することも真の
自分を見出すことも
できない。’

イイ・ カミングス

マイノリティとして生きる
ヨンス（13歳）

　　ここでは、僕の国籍と僕がそれとどう向き合ったか、について書こうと思う。

　　まずは国籍の話から。実は僕、日本で生まれて日本でこれまでずーっと暮らしてきたけれども、日本人ではなく、韓国人なんだ。いわゆる、在日韓国人ってやつ。韓国学校に行っていたり、家で韓国語を喋っていたりするわけではないから、韓国語は喋れない。まあ普通の日本人よりはできるけどね。

　　僕は小学校を卒業するまでずっと、張暎洙、というこの名前ではなくて、太田暎洙という名前で生活していた。なんでかって？通名ってやつだよ。うーん…簡単に説明すると、異国籍の人が自分たちが暮らしやすくな

るために付ける、日本風の名前。特に昔では、韓国人だというだけで多少たりとも公平には見てもらえなかったみたいだからね。僕のおじいちゃん、おばあちゃんはそう言ってた。でも僕は、中学校に入学すると同時に太田という名字を捨てた。それは、自分の本当の名前で生きたい、って思ったから。みんなには分かるかどうか分からないけど、やっぱり本当の自分として生きるってことが大事だと思ったんだ。いくら日本で生まれ育ったと言っても、僕には韓国人の血が流れているってことを知っていたし、誇りに感じていた。名字を変えるっていうのは、少し緊張するというか、恥ずかしいことではあったけれど、今では全く後悔していないよ。むしろ名字を変えて堂々とできているって感じ！小学校の時からの友達の中にあった違和感も無くなっているんじゃないかな…？もう中学校に入ってから１年半も経っているんだから。入学式のときにはすごくびっくりされたけどね。名字を変えてより深まったことと言えば、やっぱり韓国という自分の母国への愛国心だよ。在日韓国人、という日本における一種のマイノリティだということを隠さずに生きる、ということは、韓国人としての責任を背負うことになるのだからね。韓国で生まれ育つ韓国人には感じられないものを感じられているのだと思う。

　僕は今年の夏休みに、日本全国に住む在日韓国人中高生約100人で韓国へ、１週間の母国研修へ行った。みんな僕と同じように、在日韓国人というマイノリティ

として生きている仲間だ。たくさんの友達を作ることができて、彼らとはメールで連絡を取り合っているよ。また会う約束だってしている。毎日学校で一緒に勉強し、一緒に部活動に励む友達とはまた違う絆を彼らとは作り上げられたんだよ！民族的なつながりってすごいな、と僕は感じている。日本人として日本で生まれ育つのでは絶対に感じることのできないものだとも思った。

　　　また、その母国研修の中で、僕はホームステイを体験した。韓国の高校生の家に泊まらせてもらったんだ。彼女の名前はダヘ。すごく絵が上手だった。僕は日常会話ほどの韓国語もできないから、英語で彼女とコミュニケーションを取った。僕は帰国子女じゃないから英語はペラペラじゃない。けど、英語って大切だな、と改めてその時実感したよ。韓国語が喋れないまま家に行ったとき、唯一のコミュニケーション手段が英語だったからね。僕は、自分の英語が文法的にぐちゃぐちゃだと知っていながらもがむしゃらにしゃべった。そうすると不思議なことにホームステイ先の家族とお互いの思う全てのことが伝えられるようになったんだ！すごく嬉しかった！緊張しっぱなしだった僕だけれど、とても親切にして下さったし、思い出もたくさんできた。ダヘとその家族と一緒に焼き肉屋さんに行ったこと、ミョンドンという街に一緒に買い物に行ったこと。そして一番感動したのは、僕が日本に帰った後に彼女が僕にくれたメール。日本語に訳すとこんな感じ。

「ただ一つ絶対に忘れてはいけないこと、それは私たちに同じ民族の血が流れているんだ、という心の熱くなるような感情だよ。」

このメッセージは、彼女が、僕に初めて同じ民族だということを示してくれた言葉だったんだ。韓国語という母国語も喋れない韓国人に、「あなたは韓国人なんだよ」という韓国人として一番大事なことを教えてくれた彼女に感謝したい。僕はこれからずっと、一人の韓国人として堂々と生きていきたい。

　最後に、日本人に伝えたいこと、それは異民族・異国籍の人を、ステレオタイプにとらわれずに一人の人間として見てほしい、ってこと。「韓国人は〇〇だから…」だとか言うのはやめてほしい。僕自身そのような経験で嫌な思いをしたことはないけれど、きっと異国籍の人などに対して偏見を持ってしまっている大人がこの世にはたくさんいるんじゃないかと思う。大人がそのような偏見を捨てることが、日本が世界の人々に対して優しい国になるための第1歩だと思う。

'起こるべくして起こるものなど何もない：過去の障害こそが新しいスタートへと導いてくれるのだ。'

ラルフ・バルム

ずっと一緒に
ロバート（15 歳）

　　　僕はマニラのごく普通の村で母と妹と 10 年間暮らしていた。3 階建ての典型的な大きな家に住んでいた。その家のいいところは、友達や親せきなどのお客さんが泊まれて、翌日もゆっくりと過ごすことができたことだ。いつもいとこたちとテレビゲームやスポーツをしたりして、ふざけて遊んだりすることが僕たちのお気に入りだった。2 人のいとこと妹と僕の 4 人組だった。いとこの一人は僕より 2 つ年上だったから僕たちのグループのリーダーだったけれど、実際のリーダーは僕だったんじゃないかと思う。だって、僕がいつも完璧なアイデアや判断をしていたんだから。ライバル的な関係だったから、誰がリーダーかといつももめるのも当たり前だった。しょっちゅう喧嘩をしても、僕たちの友情の絆はとても強かったし、いずれにせよ、ぼくらは血がつながっている

んだ。もう一人のいとこはグループの中で一番幼く、いつも僕と一緒にいたがった。彼は僕にいろんなことを質問してきたり、スポーツでなにかすごい技を見せて、とせがんできたりした。妹はいつもグループの「仲裁役」だった。僕の年上のいとこと僕が喧嘩を始めると止めるのは彼女の役目で、決まって彼女が僕たちの不毛な争いを止めてくれたのだった。

　学校のスケジュールの関係で、いつも月に2回会っていた。外で待ち合わせをすると、いつもショッピング・モールへ行った。そこで、まずはお店を見て歩く前にどこで食べるか決めた。僕はパスタやピザが好きだから、いつもイタリアン・レストランがいいと思っていたけど、他の人たちは、中華や洋食のレストランがいいと言った。食事のあと、お店をみてまわった。僕はスポーツが大好きだからスポーツショップによく行った。従兄弟たちはテレビゲームおたくだから、いつもゲームショップやゲームセンターで過ごしていた。グループの中で妹が紅一点だったので、彼女はただみんなの行くところについて歩いていた。公園にも行って走り回ったりもした。子どもの頃大好きだったのは鬼ごっこで、よく遊んだ。僕はグループの中で足も一番早かったんだ。バスケットボールやサッカーなどのスポーツのこととなると、僕はいつでも汗を流す準備万端だった。勉強は得意じゃなかったけれど、年上のいとこが教えてくれた。彼は親切で賢かった。もう一人のいとこも優秀な生徒だったけれど、美術や音楽が苦手で、逆に妹はそれらが

得意だった。彼女はいつもピアノやリコーダーを演奏していた。年上のいとこもリコーダー、ピアノ、木琴など色々な楽器を演奏できた。僕はあまり音楽に興味はなかったけれど、それでもその頃はギターを弾いたりしていた。だから、僕たちは、素晴らしい才能にあふれたグループだと思っていた。

　そんな楽しい日々が過ぎて、父の仕事の関係で東京に引っ越すことを母が決めた。母は家族そろって生活することを願っていた。母、父、妹、そして僕だ。そのことを聞いたとき、がっかりした気持ちを笑顔で隠そうとがんばった。でも、どうして日本に引っ越さなければならないのか、と文句もたくさん言った。学校でみんなに、特にいとこたちに引っ越しを告げるのは本当につらかった。

　外国に引っ越してしまうというのは、彼らにとって相当ショックだったし、本当に悲しませてしまった。マニラを出発する日、友達、特にいとこたちにさよならを言うのは本当につらかった。新しい学校のお休みにはフィリピンに帰ってくると約束もした。飛行機の中でも、置いてきた友達やいとこたちのことを考えつづけ、ちょっぴり泣いた。

　日出る国日本に着くと、父が空港の到着ロビーで待っていてくれた。新しい家に着くまで２時間かかった。東京での家をみて、うれしかったし、ちょっと興奮したけれど、同時にマニラでの家のことも思った。

転んで、学んで、立ち上がる

新しい学校での初日は、新しい友達にあって本当にシャイになってしまった。それぞれ違う国からきている彼らにどんな風に話しかけたらいいのかもわからず、毎日大変だった。これは、僕の新しい学校が色々な国の子どもが勉強しにきているインターーナショナル・スクールだったからだ。そして、今の学校に来て 20 日くらいたったころ、ずっとたくさんのクラスメートと話せるようになり、居心地よく感じるようになり始めた。

　　　1 か月もたつと、マニラでの暮らしのことを考えていない自分に気付いた。そして、その頃にはもう日本での新しいスタートで自分の新しい目標を見出していたのだ。僕の家族は冬休みと夏休みに 2 週間、友達や親せきに会いにフィリピンへ帰った。たとえ離れて暮らしていても、僕たちのグループの絆は今までにも増して固いと実感した。どんなにお互いが遠く離れても、僕たちの関係はどんなことにも揺らぐことなく変わらないとわかったんだ。

‘自分の考え方をかえなさい。そうすれば世界が変わる。’

ノーマン・ビンセント・ピール

先生こわい
マニヤ（12歳）

　　すべては数年前、私の友達と私が前の学校に入っ
たときに始まった。まだ幼かったので、私の友達は誰か
れかまわず話しかけ、誰とでも交流することが好きだっ
た。でも、私は違った。私はとてもシャイで、どちらか
というと一人でいることの方が好きだった。ちょうど学
年の始まりのときだったのでクラスメートには馴染んだ
のだが、先生たちとは違った。先生に何か聞かれると、
私の返事はうなずくか首を振るかのどちらかだった。何
かわからないことがあった時などは、聞くのがこわくて
間違えたことをしてしまったりした。友達にどうしてそ
んなに先生たちのことを怖がるのか聞かれた時、私は
「先生はなんだか私のことを不安にさせるし、私のこと
を嫌いなんじゃないかって思う時だってある。」と答え
た。

　　しかし、学期がすすむにつれ、先生たちは生徒全
員を呼んで、宿題やその他のことで何か困っていること
はないか、私たちを手伝えることはないか、と聞くこと
になった。こういうとき、私は友達にこんな風なことを

転んで、学んで、立ち上がる

聞いた。「私、何を聞かれるんだろう？！」とか、「もしこんなことを聞かれたらなんて答えたらいいんだろう…」とか。半年ほど経ったころ、自分が怖気づかずに先生と話せるような方法を見出そうとしていることに気付いた。そして、自分が恐れていることを乗り越えるために小さな一歩を踏み出していることに気付いたのだ。最初それに気付いたのは、授業中に先生がした質問にできるだけ詳しくきちんと答えようとしたときだった。

　　　それから自分自身に自信がつき始めたことを感じることができるようになり、先生にも何が本当に自分を悩ませているのかを話すことができるようになった。そしてとうとう自分から質問したり本当の会話ができたりするようになったのだ。このことは、勉強だけでなく、いろいろなことで私によい結果をもたらした。授業の内容がずっとよく理解できるようになったし、先生からもたくさん褒められるようになった。

　　　あれから何年も経ってさらに成長した今では、先生たちともよくやりとりできるようになり、クラスでも一番にぎやかで一番明るい生徒の一人になっている。

‘人生において恐れる
ものなど何もない。理
解すればよいだけのこ
とである。’

マリー・キュリー

人前で話すこと恐怖症
ジェイジェイ（12 歳）

　　小さい頃から人前で話すのが得意でなかった。スピーチ原稿を書いたり、プレゼンテーションの計画を立てたりすることは本当に好きなのだが。人前に出て話し始めようとすると固まってしまい、自信が消え失せてしまう。自分の恐怖心を乗り越えようとしているけれど、傍目から見るほど簡単なことじゃない。感じ方や自然に出る行動をコントロールすることはできない。なぜこの恐怖心を克服したいかというと、私にとっての一番の理由は、自分のプレゼンテーションへの影響だ。どんなに素晴らしいスピーチを用意しても聴衆に言いたいことが伝わらないのだから。

転んで、学んで、立ち上がる

それほど大したことではないように聞こえるかもしれないが 、このせいで私は色々ことができずにいるのだ。コンサートで何か発表することすらできないし、校外活動も限られてくる。
幼かったころは、それほど多くの成績を左右するような大事なプレゼンテーションやたくさんの人の前でのプレゼンテーションの機会もなかったため、大して大きな問題ではなかった。そのため、自分でも自分が抱えているこの問題のことをほとんど忘れてしまっていた。

　今年から、クラスの前で説明することを含む、たくさんの重要な課題が出されるようになった。最初にこのことを聞いたとき、パニックを起こした。そして、やらなければならないプレゼンテーションの当日になると、どんなにたくさん練習していても本当に緊張してしまうのだ。

　一番最近のプロジェクト課題では、クラス全員の前に出てスピーチをしなければならなかった。これは課題のために重要な要件だったし、これで先生の採点が左右されるということでひどく緊張していた。先生がプレゼンテーションをするようにと私の名前を呼んだとき、私は震えていた。私自分のスピーチを全部暗記していて、何を言えばいいかもはっきりわかっていたので、なぜそんなに緊張しているのか自分でも不思議だった。
ところが驚いたことに、壇上にあがると少しも緊張を感じなくなっていた。スピーチはまるで風のようになめらかで、自分でも上出来だと思った。先生も素晴らしい自信をもってスピーチできていたと言ってくれて、自分で

もそんなにうまくできたとはわからず、びっくりしてしまった。

　この経験をしてから、今では自分をうまくコントロールできるようになり、間違いをしないように念を入れるようになったので、他のときも緊張することはなくなった。恐怖心を克服したことは自分でも本当に誇りに思っている。今でもスピーチをしなければならないときに飛び上がって喜ぶということはないけれど、恐怖で震えるなんていうこともなくなった。

'勇気の持ちように
よって人生は伸びた
り縮んだりする。'

アナイス・ニン

慈善団体ガワド・カリンガについて

　　ガワド・カリンガ（GK）は、カルーカン・シティのバゴン・シランの元不良グループメンバー127人の青少年犯罪者によるユースキャンプに端を発する。1996年から1999年、ソーシャルエンジニアリングが始まった。不良メンバーたちに教育や訓練を与え、最初のGKハウスがある家族のために建てられた。2000年にはガワド・カリンガがついに発足。シェルターなどのいくつかのプログラムが始まり、これがのちに8つの「GK国」に支部を置く組織としてのスタートとなった。

　　『ガワド・カリンガは現在、フィリピンおよびその他インドネシア、カンボジア、パプアニューギニアなどの発展途上国のほぼ1700地域において活動をおこなっている。今日では、フィリピン人独自の精神「バヤニハン」（仲間のためにいかなる重荷も共有していこうというもの）を復活させることで、フィリピンにおける関係修復、貧富格差是正や政府・民間企業間の橋渡し、を具現化する大きな流れとなっている。信仰への強い信念の上に立って、GKはすべてのフィリピン人を国のためのヒーローとすることで彼らの中の愛国心を取り戻している。それは「バヤニ」と呼ばれる、「新しい家、新しい人生、新しい国」に貢献するものである。よりよい場所を求めて国を喜んで出ていく人々が多い時勢に、ガワ

ド・カリンガは、この素晴らしい国を維持しフィリピン人としての誇りを取り戻す、というフィリピンの人々の夢に希望の光を与えたのだ。』(gk1world.com)

ガワド・カリンガの創始者はアントニオ・メロト氏。彼は「ティト（おじさんの意）・トニー」として知られ、1950年1月17日に生まれた。『幼くしてすでに彼は、貧困にあえぐ荒れ果てた生活を目の当たりにしていた。彼の家は海岸沿いの不法居住者の地域に程近く、そこは1950年代でさえすでに貧困が明らかな状態であった。』(gk1world.com) 1995年、彼はバゴン・シランで青少年向けの活動を始めようと思い立ち、これがガワド・カリンガとしてのちに知られる組織団体のさきがけとなった。

この組織は子どもや大人の生活の向上を目指すもので、たとえば、GK施設内の障害児たちにインフラ設備、価値形成プログラム、また建築活動のノウハウを与えるものなどがある。

これが、私がこの組織団体を選んだひとつの理由である。この組織は、十分な生活物資もなく貧困にあえぐ人々に手を差しのべている。しかもその多くは私と同じような若者たちであり、GKは彼らに人生をやり直すチャンスを与えてくれているのだ。

本書の売上による収益金はすべて、ガワド・カリンガ施設内における人々の生活向上のための青少年プロジェクトに寄付されます。